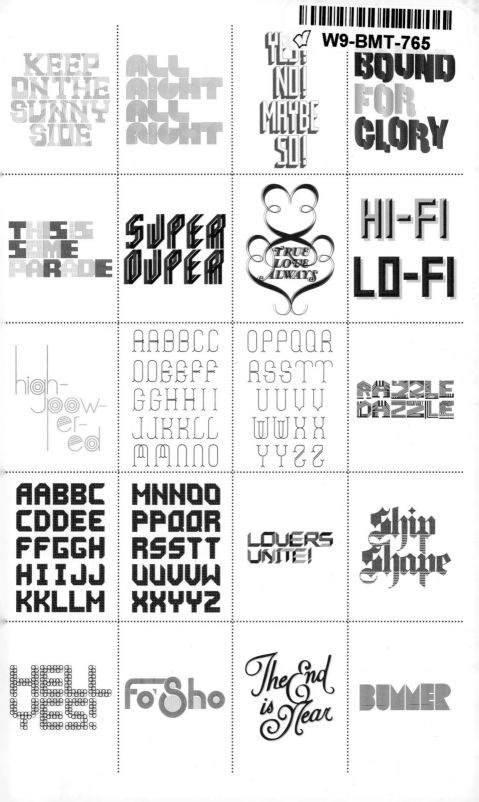

Welcome to the World of Iron-Ons!

With these decal-based iron-on transfers, you can create one-of-a-kind wearable art and gifts featuring eye-catching art and alphabets. Inside, you'll find twenty pages of graphics that can be mixed and matched to create designs for T-shirts, tote bags, pillowcases, hats, and any other fabric surface you can dream of.

Using iron-on decals is simple and fun. All you need is a hot, high-quality iron, a steady hand, fabric, and a flat, hard surface. But if you're new to iron-ons, or just need a refresher, there are a few things you should know before you begin.

Choosing Your Fabric

Iron-on transfers can be applied to most cotton-based fabric, but they work best on smooth, light-colored material, such as a T-shirt, tea towel, or handkerchief. While you can apply a transfer to dark-colored fabrics, they will not appear as vibrant as they will on light-colored material. Avoid applying transfers to rough or textured materials (such as heavy canvas) as the bumps and ridges in the fabric will affect the quality of the transfer.

The designs in this book can be used in a variety of ways. There are stand-alone graphics that you can cut out and use as the centerpiece for a T-shirt and there are alphabets, from which you can make your own words and phrases. Be sure to plan your design ahead of time by mapping it out on the garment you plan to use. Remember the old maxim of "measure twice, cut once," when planning your design.

Your Iron

Once you've prepared your design, the next step is to apply it to your garment. Use a hot, high-quality iron on its highest heat setting. Make sure to turn the steam feature off and remove any water from the iron's reservoir. Before you begin to apply the transfers, the iron should be HOT—heat and even pressure are the keys to a quality iron-on transfer, so let the iron heat up for at least five minutes.

Your Workspace

Choose a smooth, hard surface as your workspace, such as a worktable or bench, a Formica countertop, or piece of smooth plywood. Don't use an ironing board, as it won't hold the necessary heat. Cover your workspace with an old sheet, pillowcase, or other smooth fabric. Make sure there are no wrinkles or ridges in your workspace.

Time to Iron-On!

1. Iron your garment to make sure there are no wrinkles and lay it flat on your workspace. Arrange your design on your fabric transfer-side down (remember that the images reverse in the transfer, so if you're using letters to spell out a word or phrase, make sure you've planned it out correctly).

2. Lay your hot iron down on the center of your transfer and apply even pressure using both hands. Move your iron over the transfer in slow circles from the outer edges towards the center of the transfer, maintaining even pressure throughout the process. The transfer should start right away as the glue from the decals begins to merge with the fabric. The entire process should take roughly 2 to 4 minutes, depending on the heat of your iron and the quality of the fabric.

With decal-based transfers, a little finesse goes a long way. Too much time under the iron can burn and crack the decal, too little will make it difficult to remove—it takes patience and practice, especially if you are working over a large area. Work in stages!

3. Once your transfer is complete, remove from heat and let the transfer sheet cool before carefully removing from your garment in one even motion.

4. Enjoy your creation!

Iron-On Tips and Tricks:
As you flip through the designs you'll notice all the text is backward. That's because the text will reverse when you iron it on. If you can't tell what a design says, simply hold it up to a mirror for an instant translation or refer to the handy thumbnails at the front of pad.

Unless you consider yourself an iron-on expert, do a few tests on spare garments before creating your iron-on masterpiece. Iron temperatures vary and different fabrics react differently to the heat transfer, so there will always be some trial and error that you will need to work through.

Don't "peek" by lifting the transfer sheet before your transfer is complete. Even a slight shift of the transfer sheet can result in a blurred or double-image of the transfer.

To easily apply the proper amount of pressure (30 to 50 pounds) try working on a surface lower than a conventional tabletop so that you can use your upper body to add weight to the iron without too much effort.

Be careful! Irons are hot and, at least during the process, your garment will be hot and the transfer sheets will be hot. Always use caution—and remember that the transfer images can bleed through your garment (and on to your workspace) if left under the heat too long.

Washing and Care of Your Iron-On Creation
With a little extra care, your iron-on transfer should weather the laundry cycle well. Turn your garment inside out and wash it on the gentle cycle in cold water using color-safe detergent. On your first wash, be sure to remove from the washer promptly to help prevent color bleeding. Air-dry or run through a dryer on low heat.

Who Made *Hot Type*
The graphic design studio MacFadden & Thorpe was founded by Brett MacFadden and Scott Thorpe. They have designed projects for Chronicle Books, the *New York Times*, *Dwell*, AIGA, SFMOMA, and more. Scott and Brett both live in San Francisco, CA and chronicle their work here: www.macfaddenandthorpe.com.

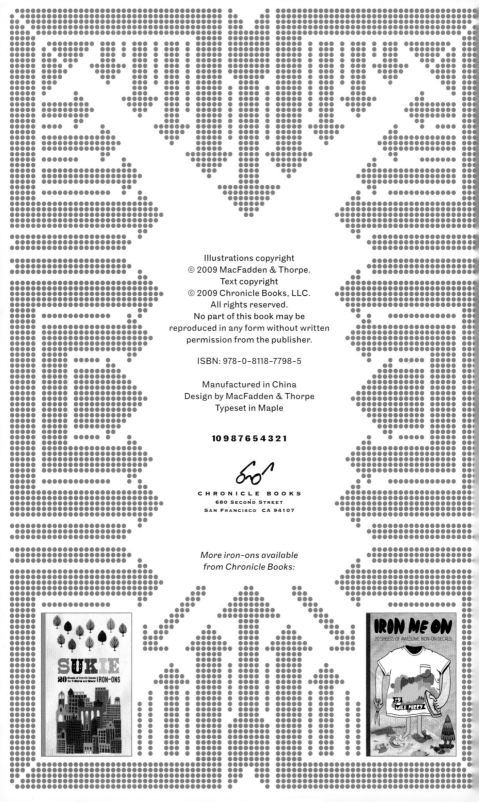

ISBN: 978-0-8118-7798-5

Manufactured in China
Design by MacFadden & Thorpe
Typeset in Maple

10 9 8 7 6 5 4 3 2 1

CHRONICLE BOOKS
680 SECOND STREET
SAN FRANCISCO CA 94107

*More iron-ons available
from Chronicle Books:*

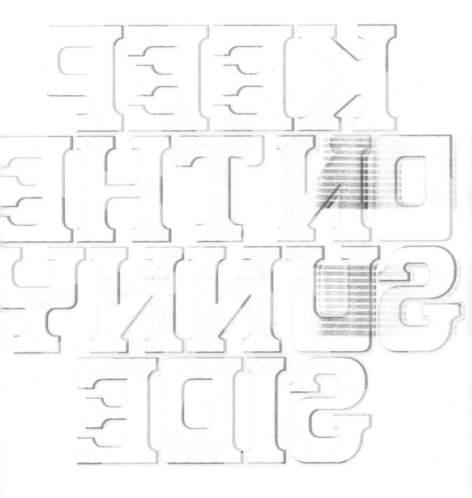

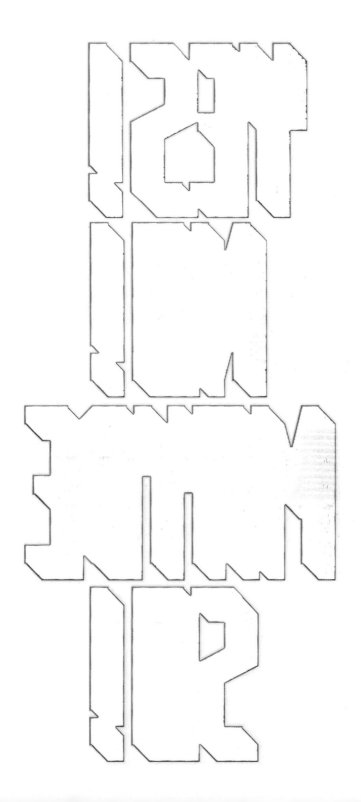

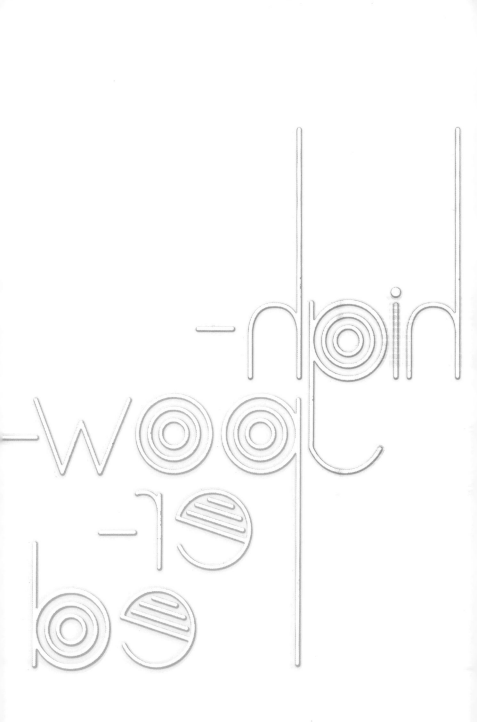

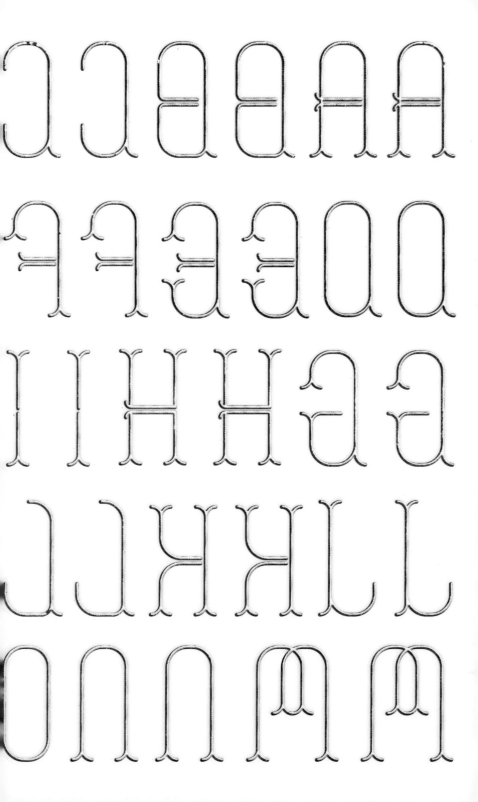

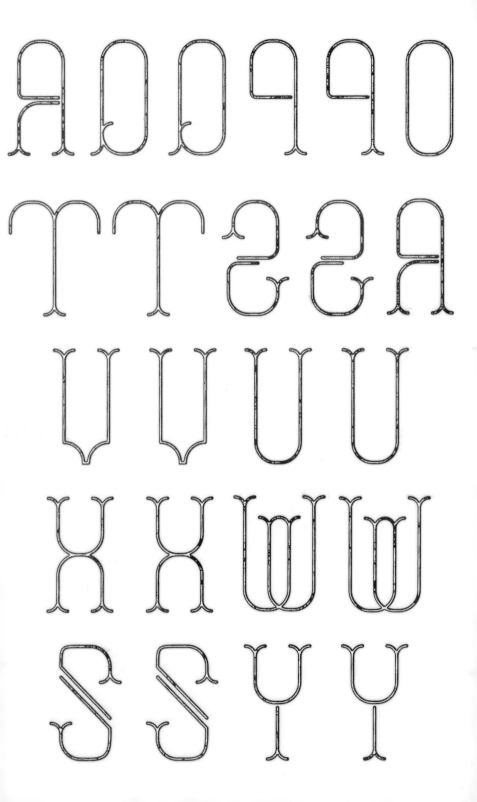

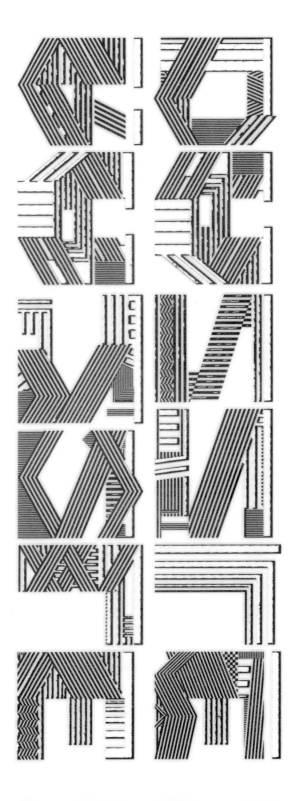

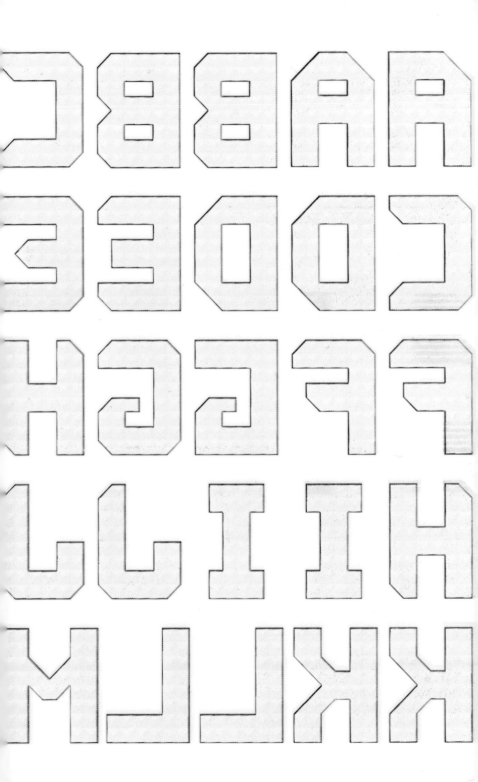

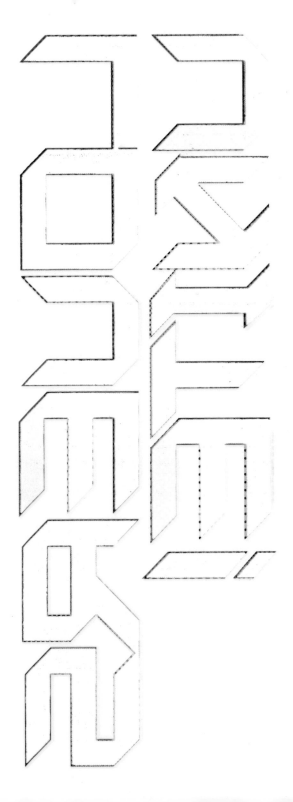

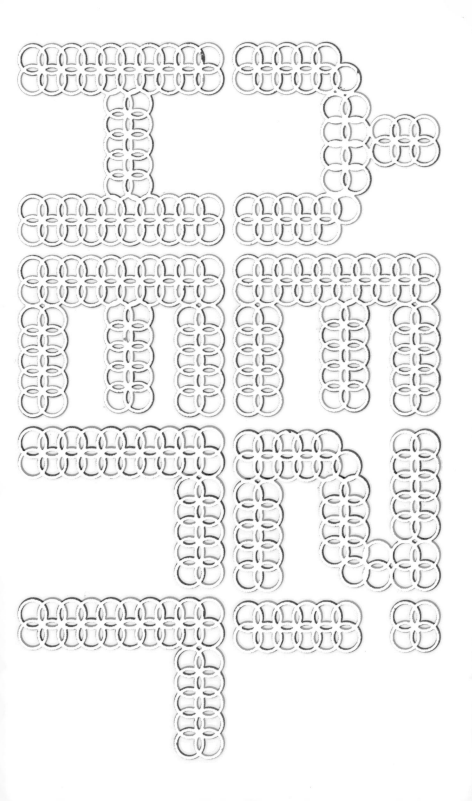

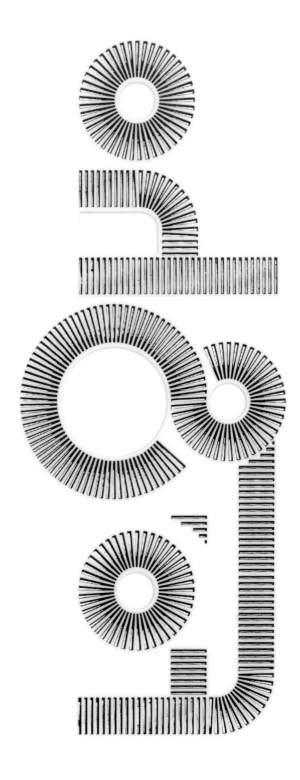